Wolfgang Amadeus Mozart

Clarinet Concerto in A major / A-Dur
K 622

Edited by / Herausgegeben von
Richard Clarke

EULENBURG

EAS 136
ISBN 978-3-7957-6536-1
ISMN M-2002-2360-6

Edition based on Eulenburg Study Score ETP 778

Ernst Eulenburg Ltd
48 Great Marlborough Street
London W1F 7BB

Contents / Inhalt

Preface V

Vorwort IX

I. Allegro 1 Track 1

II. Adagio 42 Track 2

III. Rondo. Allegro 50 Track 3

Preface

The Clarinet Concerto is the last major work Mozart lived to complete. His next project was the D minor *Requiem*, left unfinished at his death on 5th December 1791. In a letter to his wife Constanze, written between 7th and 8th October of that last year, Mozart mentions that he has just 'orchestrated almost the whole Rondò' of the Concerto, which would suggest that by this stage the work was substantially complete. Many commentators have marvelled at the speed with which Mozart appears to have composed the Concerto: evidence suggests that most of the work was done during the first week of October. However he was not working from scratch. At some stage, possibly a year or two earlier, Mozart had begun a Concerto in G major for basset horn (despite its name, this is actually the tenor instrument of the clarinet family). The detailed draft score extends to 199 bars and is very close in substance to the first movement orchestral and solo expositions plus the beginning of the development of K 622.

It was not unusual for Mozart to sketch out the beginning of a work and then put it to one side, taking it up some time later when an opportunity for performance arose. The Piano Concerto in A major, K 488, for example, was begun 1784, with oboes instead of the now familiar clarinets. Mozart completed it in 1786, adjusting the orchestration to suit the forces available – any opportunity to use clarinets was welcomed by Mozart. In the case of the Clarinet Concerto the stimulus was a request from the great Viennese virtuoso Anton Stadler, who gave the first performance in Prague on 16th October, just over a week after the above-quoted letter to Constanze. Stadler was one of the musicians Mozart admired most warmly. The two men had met shortly after Mozart had arrived in Vienna in 1781. Stadler's reputation was already impressive: in that same year the Emperor had publicly described him as 'indispensable'. Stadler's phenomenal technical agility was matched by an expressive musicality which marked him out amongst his peers. A contemporary critic observed that 'one would never have thought that a clarinet could imitate the human voice to such perfection'.

Such playing would have appealed strongly to Mozart. As the fortepianist and Mozart authority Robert Levin aptly remarks, there are marked 'anthropomorphic' qualities to the solo writing in Mozart's concertos, inviting direct comparison with his operatic and concert arias. 'Both domains demonstrate Mozart's genius in character portrayal while reconciling virtuosity with the needs of dramatic expression; both deploy prodigious melodic invention, a fluid rhythmic language and a voluptuous orchestra fabric.'[1] In these respects Stadler's playing probably came closer to Mozart's ideals than anyone else's – except perhaps his own. Stadler took part in the premieres of a number of important Mozart works, in all of which he appears to have given special satisfaction to the composer. In 1784, the two men played together in the first performance of the Quintet for piano and winds, K 452, which the delighted Mozart

[1] 'Concertos' in *The Mozart Compendium*, ed. H.C. Robbins Landon, London, 1990, p263.

then pronounced 'the best thing' he had written. Stadler's performance of the clarinet part may well have influenced that slightly surprising judgement - surprising because by this stage Mozart had already composed his magnificent Mass in C minor, K 427, and the first three of his six great 'Haydn' quartets, K 387 in G major, K 421 in D minor, and K 428 in E flat major, widely counted amongst his finest achievements, and all of them more ambitious technically and in 'character portrayal' than the Quintet.

So it is easy to understand how the chronically overworked Mozart might still have leapt at the opportunity to rework and complete his earlier basset-horn concerto draft for Stadler in October 1791. The result was more or less the Clarinet Concerto as we know it today, though with one significant difference. The instrument Stadler played – and indeed had personally devised – had a slightly deeper range than the modern clarinet in A, taking it down to a written low C (concert A). Though Stadler had great success with the instrument, it soon fell out of favour (no examples of Stadler's deeper A clarinet have survived), to be replaced by the familiar clarinets in A and B flat. The version of the score that has been familiar for the best part of two centuries is a reworking for the modern clarinet in A with some of the deeper bass notes transposed. Almost certainly this arrangement was not made by Mozart himself. In March 1802, a review of the first edition of the parts of the Clarinet Concerto, as published by Breitkopf und Härtel, appeared in the *Allgemeine Musikalische Zeitung*. Here the unnamed critic – while praising the music generally – complains about the new version of the solo part, comparing it unfavourably with what he claims to have heard Stadler play. 'Whereas currently such clarinets descending to low C can still be counted among the rare instruments, one is indebted to the editors, who spared no pains in making these transpositions and alterations for the normal clarinet, although the concerto has not exactly gained thereby. It might have been better to have published it entirely according to the original, and to have rendered the transpositions and alterations at most by small notes'.

Tradition has a way of sanctioning all manner of oddities and anomalies in works of art, so it is perhaps unsurprising that critics in later generations were not inclined to find fault with the reworked clarinet part in the familiar edition of K 622 – until, that is, the rise of the 'period instrument' movement in the 1980s inevitably brought the issue to the fore again. Alas, Mozart's original manuscript had long disappeared, and with it any part material used by Stadler for the 1791 first performance. Constanze Mozart had no doubt at all where the blame lay, accusing Stadler of pawning it – along with several other Mozart manuscripts – for an unimpressive 73 ducats. However, the sketch score for the G major basset-horn concerto has survived, and it gives several crucial clues as to how the original solo part might have differed from the version hallowed by tradition. Take the figure in bars 94–5 of the first movement for example: when one knows that the clarinet Mozart wrote for could reach down to low written C, the awkwardness of the movement from the last three quavers of bar 94 to the semiquaver figures of bar 95 virtually leaps off the page. Even without the evidence of the original basset-horn draft, a simple analogy with bars 96–7 would be enough to indicate what Mozart's original intentions must surely have been. It is hard to believe that Mozart – even under extreme pressure – would have settled for a crude part-transposition like the one perpetuated since the first edition. Another striking example comes at the climax of the Adagio (bars 55 *et seq*). Given an instrument like Stadler's, with an extra major third in the bass register, there would have been no need to break up the demi-semiquaver arpeggios on the second beats of bar 55 and 57. A continuous upward movement starting on low C is more elegant, and it allows the soloist to demonstrate a far wider range of tone colour at this dramatic high point of the movement.

Since interest in the nature of the original Clarinet Concerto began to re-awaken in recent times, attempts have been made to reconstruct the solo part as Mozart might have intended it, and clarinets have been built with the same extended bass compass as Stadler's instrument. The result has been christened the 'basset clarinet', and has become increasingly popular in both the concert hall and the recording studio: so much so that it now enjoys almost equal popularity with the modern A clarinet. However, there is no sign that the latter instrument is in serious decline in performances of K 622. Indeed the clarinettist Maximiliano Martin has demonstrated in his recording (Linn CKD 273) that, with the benefit of scholarly hindsight, the solo part can easily be adjusted on the modern clarinet to remove some of the crudities present in the old edition.

Rightly or wrongly, the fact that the Clarinet Concerto is Mozart's last completed major work has inevitably affected the way it has been performed and discussed. The scholar H.C. Robbins Landon was clearly not expecting any serious disagreement when he wrote, in the mid 1950s, that 'no other work by Mozart is more imbued with that final, quiet resignation… The concerto is Mozart's farewell to the realms of pure music'[2]. Robbins Landon goes on to state that 'by October [Mozart] must have guessed the extent of his illness', but there is no solid evidence to support that hypothesis, or that he had any serious intuition that he was nearing the end of his life. By the time Robbins Landon returned to the subject three decades later in his important study *1791: Mozart's Last Year*, he had revised his opinion substantially, arguing instead that Mozart was on the brink of a 'new era'[3], buoyed up by the recent huge success of his opera *Die Zauberflöte*, K 620, and looking forward eagerly to his promised appointment as Kapellmeister at St Stephen's Cathedral, Vienna, on the death or retirement of the then incumbent, Leopold Hofmann. Certainly there are parts in the Clarinet Concerto – particularly in the central *Adagio* – which show a distinctly melancholy cast of expression. Interestingly, performance on the basset clarinet, with the solo range extended downwards accordingly, does tend to bring a more sombre colouring to other passages. However it would be just as easy to identify a 'final, quiet resignation' in the slow movement and finale introduction of the String Quintet in G minor, K 516, written four years earlier. The emotional colouring of both these works may have more to do with a possible depressive tendency in Mozart's character than with any alleged mystical intuition of approaching death in October 1791.

Nevertheless, the Clarinet Concerto's mythological status as Mozart's 'farewell to the realms of pure music' has proved enduring and influential. Perhaps the quasi-sacred aura associated with the work helps explain the puzzling fact that so few lastingly successful clarinet concer-

[2] 'The Concertos (2)' in *The Mozart Companion*, ed h.c. Robbins Landon & Donald Mitchell, London, 1956, p279.
[3] H.C. Robbins Landon: *Mozart's Last Year*, London 1988, p147

tos have been composed since Mozart's death, despite the instrument's eminent suitability as a virtuoso soloist on the large concert stage. Undeniably the modern repertoire is significantly richer in chamber music featuring solo clarinet than in major clarinet concertos. Moreover the most successful works for clarinet and orchestra, from the concertos of Weber and Bernhard Henrik Crusell to Harrison Birtwistle's *Melencolia I*, rarely betray any signs of engaging with the Mozart Concerto as a model. A possible exception is the opening movement of Aaron Copland's Clarinet Concerto (1947–8), whose sweetly nostalgic tone and lyrical use of wide intervallic leaps could be said to show Mozart's influence. A more specific invocation however can be found towards the end of the one-movement Clarinet Concerto by Carl Nielsen (1928), written at a time when its composer was haunted by thoughts of his own mortality. At Fig 41 (*Poco adagio*) in the Nielsen Concerto the clarinet (also in A) plays a melodic idea centred on the same two notes (concert G and C) with which the solo exposition of the Mozart Concerto begins – an idea which could with more justification be said to express 'final, quiet resignation' than anything in K 622. If this is a direct tribute to Mozart's Clarinet Concerto, perhaps its very nature – an offering from one composer nearing death to another – explains why such acts of homage have been relatively rare.

Stephen Johnson

Vorwort

Das Klarinettenkonzert ist das letzte größere Werk, dass Mozart vor seinem Tod vollendete. Sein nächstes, das *Requiem* in d-Moll, blieb durch seinen Tod am 5. Dezember 1791 unvollendet. In einem Brief an Konstanze, der zwischen dem 7. und 8. Oktober desselben Jahres geschrieben war, erwähnt Mozart das Konzert, „Instrumentierte ich fast das ganze Rondò", und man kann daher annehmen, dass da das Konzert praktisch fertig war. Viele Reporter staunten über die Geschwindigkeit, mit der Mozart das Konzert scheinbar komponierte: alles deutet darauf hin, dass das meiste in der ersten Oktoberwoche fertiggestellt war. Allerdings musste er nicht bei null anfangen. Vor einiger Zeit, vielleicht ein oder zwei Jahre zuvor, hatte er ein Konzert in G-Dur für Bassetthorn angefangen (trotz des Namens gehört es zur Klarinettenfamilie, als deren Tenorinstrument). Der detaillierte Partiturentwurf macht 199 Takte aus und ähnelt im Wesen dem ersten Satz für Orchester- und Soloexpositionen sowie dem Anfang der Durchführung von KV. 622.

Es war nicht ungewöhnlich, dass Mozart den Anfang eines Werkes entwarf und dann zur Seite legte, um es später, wenn die Möglichkeit einer Aufführung bestand, wieder hervorzuholen. Das Klavierkonzert in A-Dur, KV. 488, ist ein Beispiel, das 1784 begonnen wurde, für Oboen an Stelle der jetzigen Klarinetten. Mozart vollendete es 1786 und glich die Instrumentierung den gegebenen Umständen an – er freute sich über jede Gelegenheit, Klarinetten verwenden zu können. Die Anregung für das Klarinettenkonzert kam in Form einer Bitte des großen Wiener Virtuosen Anton Stadlers, der es am 16. Oktober in Prag aus der Taufe hob, gerade eine Woche nach dem oben erwähnten Brief an Konstanze. Mozart bewunderte Stadler sehr. 1781 hatten sich die beiden kurz getroffen, nachdem Mozart nach Wien gekommen war. Damals war Stadlers Ruf bereits beeindruckend: im selben Jahr hatte der Kaiser ihn als „unentbehrlich" bezeichnet. Stadlers phänomenale Technik war mit einer ausdrucksstarken Musikalität gepaart, die ihn von seinen Musikerkollegen abstechen ließ. Ein zeitgenössischer Rezensent schrieb: „Hätt's nicht gedacht, daß ein Klarinet menschliche Stimme so täuschend nachahmen könnte".

Mozart war für solches Spielen äußerst empfänglich. Robert Levin, Fortepianist und Mozart Autorität, meint treffend, es gäbe markante „anthropomorphische" Qualitäten in den Solos von Mozarts Konzerten, die zu direkten Vergleichen mit seinen Opern- und Konzertarien einluden. „Beide Sphären zeigen Mozarts Genie als Charakterporträtist, indem er Virtuosität mit den Notwendigkeiten dramatischen Ausdrucks vereint; in beiden Fällen gibt es unglaubliche melodische Erfindungen, eine fließende, rhythmische Sprache und ein üppiges Orchestergefüge".[1] Diesbezüglich kam Stadlers Spiel wahrscheinlich Mozarts Ideal näher als das irgendeines anderen – außer vielleicht seinem eigenen. Stadler spielte in etlichen, wichtigen

[1] „Concertos", in *The Mozart Compendium*, Hg. H. C. Robbins Landon, London, 1990, S. 263.

Mozartpremieren, und immer dürfte es zu des Komponisten äußerster Zufriedenheit gewesen sein. 1784 spielten die beiden zusammen in der ersten Aufführung des Quintetts für Klavier und Bläser, KV. 452, und das veranlasste den erfreuten Mozart zu der Bemerkung, das wäre „das Beste", was er je geschrieben hätte. Stadlers Ausführung der Klarinettenstimme könnte wohl das etwas überraschende Urteil beeinflusst haben - überraschend deshalb, weil Mozart zu dieser Zeit schon seine herrliche Messe in c-Moll, KV. 427, und die ersten drei seiner großen Haydn Quartette – KV. 387 in G-Dur, KV. 421 in d-Moll und KV. 428 in Es-Dur, weithin mit zu seinen Meisterwerken zählend – komponiert hatte; sie alle sind technisch und in der „Charakterzeichnung" ambitionierter als das Quintett.

Es ist daher leicht zu begreifen, dass der ständig überarbeitete Mozart auch diese Gelegenheit beim Schopf fasste, seinen früheren Entwurf für das Bassetthorn-Konzert wieder aufzugreifen, es umarbeitete und im Oktober 1791 für Stadler fertig stellte. Das Resultat war so ziemlich genau das Klarinettenkonzert, das wir heute kennen, obwohl mit einem bedeutenden Unterschied. Stadlers Klarinette – die er selbst entworfen hatte – reichte etwas tiefer als die moderne A-Klarinette, hinunter bis zum geschriebenen tiefen C (klingendes A). Trotz Stadlers großem Erfolg auf dem Instrument kam es bald aus der Mode (es sind keine Beispiele von Stadlers tieferer A-Klarinette überliefert) und wurde von den heute bekannten A- und B- Klarinetten abgelöst. Die seit fast zwei Jahrhunderten bekannte Partiturfassung ist eine Überarbeitung für die moderne A-Klarinette mit einigen der tieferen Bassnoten transponiert. Höchstwahrscheinlich stammt diese Bearbeitung nicht von Mozart selbst. Eine Rezension der ersten Ausgabe der Stimmen des Klarinettenkonzerts – hgg. von Breitkopf & Härtel – erschien 1802 in der *Allgemeinen Musikalischen Zeitung*. Dort beschwert sich der anonyme Kritiker – obwohl er die Musik im Allgemeinen lobt – über die neue Fassung der Solostimme, die er ungünstig mit dem Spiel Stadlers, den er angeblich gehört hatte, vergleicht. „Da es heutzutage nur wenige Klarinetten gibt, die bis zum tiefen C hinunter reichen, ist den Herausgebern zu danken, die keine Mühe scheuten, die Transponierungen und Veränderungen für eine normale Klarinette anzugeben, obwohl man nicht sagen kann, dass das Konzert hierdurch besser geworden wäre. Vielleicht wäre es besser gewesen, das Werk gänzlich dem Original folgend herauszugeben und die Transponierungen und Veränderungen allenfalls in kleinen Noten zu ergänzen".

Tradition kann allerlei Eigenheiten und Anomalien in Kunstwerken zulassen, daher ist es vielleicht wenig erstaunlich, dass spätere Kritiker nichts an der umgearbeiteten Klarinettenstimme in der bekannten Ausgabe von KV. 622 auszusetzen hatten – bis die aufkommende Bewegung der „Kopien alter Instrumente" in den 80er Jahren des 20. Jhs. die Sache wieder belebte. Natürlich war Mozarts ursprüngliches Manuskript längst verschollen und damit jedes Stimmenmaterial, das Stadler bei der ersten Aufführung 1791 benutzt hatte. Konstanze Mozart hatte keinen Zweifel, wo die Schuld lag, und beschuldigte Stadler, das Material – mit anderen Mozarthandschriften – um schäbige 73 Dukaten verpfändet zu haben. Der Entwurf der Partitur für das Bassetthorn Konzert in G-Dur hat allerdings überlebt und gibt uns verschiedene Hinweise, wie die ursprüngliche Solostimme sich von der traditions-geheiligten Fassung unterschieden haben mag. Z. B. die Figur in Takt 94–95 des ersten Satzes: wenn man weiß, dass die Klarinette, für die Mozart schrieb, bis zum tiefen C reichen konnte, springt die Unbeholfenheit der Bewegung von den letzten 3 Achteln in Takt 94 bis zu den Sechzehnteln in Takt 95 sofort ins Auge. Aber auch ohne den Beweis des originalen Entwurfs für Bassethorn sollte eine einfache Analogie mit den Takten 96-97 zeigen, was Mozarts ursprüngliche Absichten sicherlich gewesen wären. Es ist kaum glaubhaft, dass sich Mozart – sogar unter größtem Druck – mit einer groben Stimmtransposition zufrieden gegeben hätte wie derjenigen, die seit der ersten Ausgabe überliefert worden war. Noch ein auffallendes Beispiel findet sich am Höhepunkt des *Adagios* (Takt 55 ff.). Mit einem Instrument wie Stadlers, das eine zusätzliche große Terz im Bassbereich hatte, gäbe es keine Notwendigkeit, die Zweiunddreißigstel-Arpeggios am 2. Schlag der Takte 55 und 57 zu teilen. Eine fortlaufende Aufwärtsbewegung, angefangen am tiefen C ist viel eleganter und erlaubt dem Solisten, ein viel breiteres Tonkolorit am dramatischen Höhepunkt des Satzes vorzuführen.

Nachdem in jüngster Zeit wieder neues Interesse am Wesen des ursprünglichen Klarinettenkonzerts erwacht war, wurde auch versucht, die Solostimme wie sie Mozart beabsichtigt haben könnte, zu rekonstruieren, und es wurden Klarinetten mit dem gleichen erweiterten Bassumfang wie Stadlers Instrument gebaut. Das Resultat ist die sogenannte „Bassett-Klarinette", die im Konzertsaal und im modernen Studio immer beliebter wird: sie erfreut sich sogar solcher Beliebtheit, dass sie nun fast ebenso populär wie die A-Klarinette ist. Das heißt jedoch nicht, dass der Gebrauch der A-Klarinette bei Aufführungen von KV. 622 ernstlich gefährdet ist. Tatsächlich zeigte der Klarinettist Maximiliano Martin in seiner Aufnahme (Linn CKD 273), dass mit Hilfe der letzten wissenschaftlichen Erkenntnisse die Solostimme auf der modernen Klarinette leicht so reguliert werden kann, dass die in der alten Ausgabe vorhandenen ärgsten Grobheiten verschwinden.

Zu Recht oder Unrecht hat die Tatsache, dass das Klarinettenkonzert Mozarts letztes, vollständiges Werk ist, die Art und Weise der Aufführung und Diskussion beeinflusst. Der Gelehrte H. C. Robbins Landon erwartete bestimmt keinen Widerspruch, als er Mitte der 50er Jahre des 20. Jhs. schrieb, dass „kein anderes Mozartwerk mehr von tiefer, stiller Resignation durchtränkt ist… Das Konzert ist Mozarts Abschied vom Reich der reinen Musik".[2] Robbins Landon meint weiter, dass [Mozart] „im Oktober das Ausmaß seiner Krankheit geahnt haben musste", aber es gibt keinerlei guten Beweis für diese Annahme oder dass er eine wirkliche Intuition von seinem bevorstehenden Ende hatte. Als Robbins Landon drei Jahrzehnte später dieses Thema in seiner wichtigen Untersuchung *1791: Mozarts Letztes Jahr* wieder aufgriff, hatte er seine Meinung wesentlich geändert und argumentierte statt dessen, dass Mozart am Rand einer „neuen Schaffensperiode"[3] stand, mit neuerlichem Elan vom jüngsten, riesigen Erfolg seiner Oper *Die Zauberflöte*, KV. 620, versehen, und er erwartete freudig, die ihm versprochene Stelle als Kapellmeister des Stephansdoms in Wien anzutreten, sobald Leopold Hofmann entweder in den Ruhestand trat oder starb. Es gibt natürlich Stellen im Klarinettenkonzert, die sehr melancholische Züge aufweisen – besonders im zentralen *Adagio.* Interessanterweise bringt das Spiel auf der Bassettklarinette mit dem in die Tiefe erweiterten Solobereich ein dunkleres Kolorit auch in anderen Passagen. Andererseits

[2] „The Concertos (2)" in *The Mozart Companion*, Hg. H. C. Robbins Landon & Donald Mitchell, London, 1956, S. 279.

[3] H. C. Robbins Landon: 1791: *Mozart's Last Year*, London 1988, S. 147.

könnte man genau so gut eine „tiefe, stille Resignation“ im langsamen Satz und der letzten Einleitung des vier Jahre früher komponierten Streichquintetts in G moll, KV. 516, sehen. Die emotionale Färbung dieser beiden Werke mag mehr mit einer möglichen Tendenz zu Depressionen in Mozarts Charakter zusammenhängen als mit angeblich mystischer Intuition vom bevorstehenden Tod im Oktober 1791.

Jedenfalls hielt sich die mythologische Stellung des Klarinettenkonzerts als Mozarts „Abschied aus dem Reich der reinen Musik“ lange und hatte großen Einfluß. Die quasi-geheiligte, mit dem Werk verbundene Aura kann vielleicht den Umstand erklären, dass seit Mozarts Tod so wenige, auf Dauer erfolgreiche Klarinettenkonzerte komponiert worden sind, obwohl das Instrument allerbestens als virtuoses Soloinstrument auf einer großen Konzertbühne geeignet ist. Es gibt keinen Zweifel, dass das moderne Repertoire bedeutend reichhaltiger an Kammermusik mit Soloklarinette als an größeren Klarinettenkonzerten ist. Auch zeigen die erfolgreichsten Werke für Klarinette und Orchester – von denen Webers und Berhard Henrik Crusells bis zu Harrison Birtwistles *Melencolia I* – kaum jemals Anzeichen, dass sie Mozarts Konzert als Vorbild genommen hätten. Eine mögliche Ausnahme ist der erste Satz in Aaron Coplands Klarinettenkonzert (1947–1948), dessen lieblich-nostalgischer Ton und lyrischer Gebrauch von weiten Intervallensprüngen Mozarts Einfluss zeigen mag. Ein deutlicherer Anklang findet sich gegen Ende des einsätzigen Klarinettenkonzerts von Carl Nielsen (1928), geschrieben, als der Komponist von Gedanken an seine eigene Sterblichkeit heimgesucht war. In der Figur 41 (*Poco adagio*) des Konzerts von Nielsen spielt die Klarinette (auch in A) eine melodische Idee, die sich um die zwei gleichen Noten (klingendes G und C) bewegt, mit denen die Soloexposition von Mozarts Konzert beginnt – eine Vorstellung, von der eher gesagt werden könnte, sie drücke „tiefe, stille Resignation“ aus als alles in KV. 622. Falls hier ein direkter Tribut an Mozarts Klarinettenkonzert gezollt wird, dann erklärt sich vielleicht aus der Natur der Sache – der Ehrung eines Komponisten am Rand des Todes an einen anderen – warum solche Huldigungen ziemlich selten sind.

Stephen Johnson
Übersetzung: Burgi Hartmann

Concerto

Wolfgang Amadeus Mozart
(1756–1791)
K 622

I. Allegro

10
Fl. 1 2
Fg. 1 2
Cor. (A) 1 2
Cl. (A)
Vl. I II
Vla.
Vc. Cb.
a 2
p
f

15
Fl. 1 2
Fg. 1 2
Cor. (A) 1 2
Cl. (A)
Vl. I II
Vla.
Vc. Cb.
a 2
tr

18
Fl. 1 2
a 2
Fg. 1 2
a 2
Cor. (A) 1 2
Cl. (A)
I
Vl.
II
Vla.
Vc. Cb.

21
a 2
Fl. 1 2
a 2
Fg. 1 2
Cor. (A) 1 2
Cl. (A)
I
Vl.
II
Vla.
Vc. Cb.

25
Fl. 1 2
Fg. 1 2
Cor. (A) 1 2
Cl. (A)
I
Vl.
II
Vla.
Violoncello
Vc.
31
Fl. 1 2
Fg. 1 2
Cor. (A) 1 2
Cl. (A)
I
Vl.
II
Vla.
Tutti Bassi
Vc.
Cb.

34
Fl. 1 2
Fg. 1 2
a 2
Cor. (A) 1 2
Cl. (A)
p
I
Vl.
II
Vla.
Vc.
Cb.
39
tr

42
Fl. 1 2
Fg. 1 2
a 2
Cor. (A) 1 2
Cl. (A)
tr
f
I
Vl.
II
Vla.
Vc.
Cb.

45
a 2
Fl. 1 2
Fg. 1 2
Cor. (A) 1 2
Cl. (A)
p
I
Vl.
II
Vla.
Vc.
Cb.

Fl. 1 2
Fg. 1 2
Cor. (A) 1 2
Cl. (A)
I
Vl.
II
Vla.
Vc.
Cb.
Solo

61
Fl. 1 2
Fg. 1 2
Cor. (A) 1 2
Cl. (A)
I
Vl.
II
Vla.
Vc.
Cb.
66
Fl. 1 2
Fg. 1 2
Cor. (A) 1 2
Cl. (A)
I
Vl.
II
Vla.
Vc.
Cb.

70
Fl. 1 2
Fg. 1 2
Cor. (A) 1 2
Cl. (A)
I
Vl.
II
Vla.
Vc.
Cb.

Tutti
Solo
75
Fl. 1 2
Fg. 1 2
Cor. (A) 1 2
Cl. (A)
I
Vl.
II
Vla.
Vc.
Cb.

81
Fl. 1 2
Fg. 1 2
Cor. (A) 1 2
Cl. (A)
Vl. I
II
Vla.
Vc. Cb.
f
p

86
Fl. 1 2
Fg. 1 2
Cor. (A) 1 2
Cl. (A)
Vl. I
II
Vla.
Vc. Cb.

92
Fl. 1 2
Fg. 1 2
Cor. (A) 1 2
Cl. (A)
I
Vl.
II
Vla.
Vc.
Cb.
tr
p

97
Tutti
Solo
a 2
Fl. 1 2
Fg. 1 2
Cor. (A) 1 2
Cl. (A)
I
Vl.
II
Vla.
Vc.
Cb.
tr
f

101
Fl. 1 2
Fg. 1 2
Cor. (A) 1 2
Cl. (A)
I
Vl.
II
Vla.
Violoncello
Tutti Bassi
Vc.
Cb.
Basso
106
Fl. 1 2
Fg. 1 2
Cor. (A) 1 2
Cl. (A)
I
Vl.
II
Vla.
Violoncello
Vc.
Cb.

110
Fl. 1 2
Fg. 1 2
Cor. (A) 1 2
Cl. (A)
I
Vl.
II
Vla.
Tutti Bassi
Violoncello
Vc.
Cb.
114
Fl. 1 2
Fg. 1 2
Cor. (A) 1 2
Cl. (A)
I
Vl.
II
Vla.
Vc.

120
Fl. 1 2
Fg. 1 2
Cor. (A) 1 2
Cl. (A)
I
Vl.
II
Vla.
Violoncello
Vc.
125
Fl. 1 2
Fg. 1 2
Cor. (A) 1 2
Cl. (A)
I
Vl.
II
Vla.
Vc.
Tutti Bassi
Violoncello
Vc.
Cb.

131
Fl. 1 2
Fg. 1 2
Cor. (A) 1 2
Cl. (A)
I
Vl.
II
Vla.
Vc.
Cb.
Vc.
Tutti Bassi
tr

135
Fl. 1 2
Fg. 1 2
Cor. (A) 1 2
Cl. (A)
I
Vl.
II
Vla.
Vc.
Cb.
tr

138
Fl. 1 2
Fg. 1 2
Cor. (A) 1 2
Cl. (A)
I
Vl.
II
Vla.
Vc.
Cb.

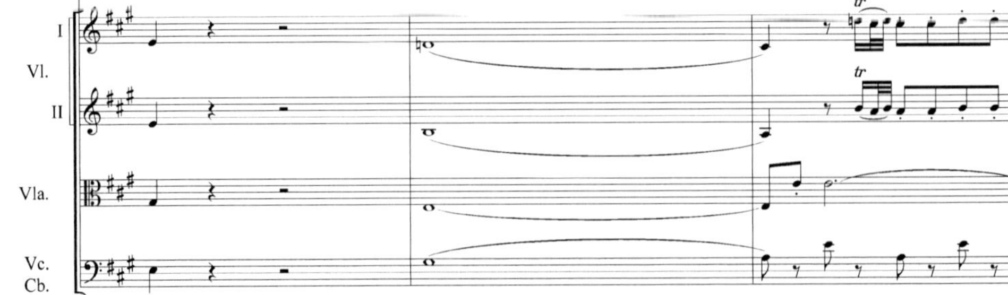
141
Fl. 1 2
Fg. 1 2
Cor. (A) 1 2
Cl. (A)
I
Vl.
II
Vla.
Vc.
Cb.
tr
tr

144
Fl. 1 2
Fg. 1 2
Cor. (A) 1 2
Cl. (A)
I
Vl.
II
Vla.
Vc.
Cb.
tr

148
Fl. 1 2
Fg. 1 2
Cor. (A) 1 2
Cl. (A)
I
Vl.
II
Vla.
Vc.
Cb.

151
Tutti
Fl. 1 2
Fg. 1 2
a 2
f
Cor. (A) 1 2
Cl. (A)
Vl. I II
cresc.
Vla.
Vc. Cb.
155

159
a 2
Fl. 1 2
a 2
Fg. 1 2
Cor. (A) 1 2
Cl. (A)
I
Vl.
II
Vla.
Vc.
Cb.

162
a 2
Fl. 1 2
a 2
Fg. 1 2
a 2
Cor. (A) 1 2
Cl. (A)
p
I
Vl.
II
p
p
Vla.
p
Vc.
Cb.
p

168
Fl. 1 2
Fg. 1 2
Cor. (A) 1 2
Cl. (A)
I
Vl.
II
Vla.
Vc.
Cb.
a 2
f
172
Solo
p

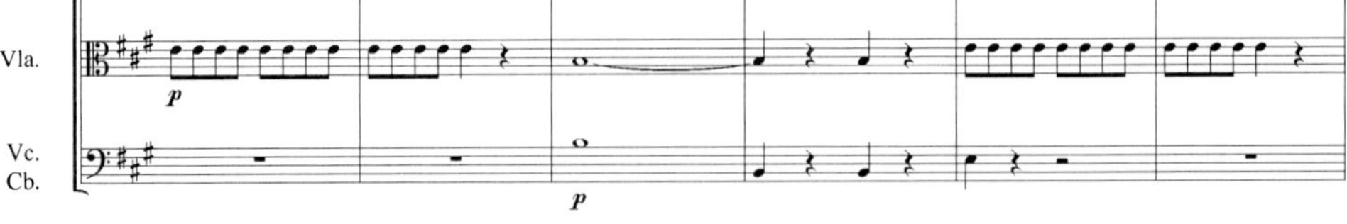

178
Fl. 1 2
Fg. 1 2
Cor. (A) 1 2
Cl. (A)
I
Vl.
II
Vla.
Vc.
Cb.
182
Fl. 1 2
Fg. 1 2
Cor. (A) 1 2
Cl. (A)
I
Vl.
II
Vla.
Vc.
Cb.

186
Fl. 1 2
Fg. 1 2
Cor. (A) 1 2
Cl. (A)
I
Vl.
II
Vla.
Vc.
Cb.
192
Tutti
Solo
a 2
f
p

198
Fl. 1 2
Fg. 1 2
a 2
Cor. (A) 1 2
p
Cl. (A)
I
Vl.
II
Vla.
Vc.
Cb.
202
Fl. 1 2
Fg. 1 2
Cor. (A) 1 2
Cl. (A)
I
Vl.
II
Vla.
Violoncello
Vc.

208
Fl. 1 2
Fg. 1 2
Cor. (A) 1 2
Cl. (A)
Vl. I II
Vla.
Vc.
Tutti Bassi
Vc. Cb.
212
a 2
f
a 2
f
Fl. 1 2
Fg. 1 2
Cor. (A) 1 2
Cl. (A)
Vl. I II
Vla.
Vc. Cb.

216
a 2
Fl. 1 2
a 2
Fg. 1 2
Cor. (A) 1 2
Cl. (A)
I
Vl.
II
p
p
Vla.
p
Vc.
Cb.
p

222
Fl. 1 2
p
cresc.
Fg. 1 2
p
cresc.
a 2
Cor. (A) 1 2
p
cresc.
Cl. (A)
tr
tr
tr
I
Vl.
II
f
f
Vla.
cresc.
Vc.
Cb.
cresc.

Tutti
227
a 2
Fl. 1 2
f
Fg. 1 2
1.
p
Cor. (A) 1 2
Cl. (A)
Vl. I II
Vla.
Vc.
Cb.

231
Fl. 1 2
Fg. 1 2
Cor. (A) 1 2
Cl. (A)
Vl. I II
Vla.
Vc.
Cb.
a 2
f

235
Fl. 1 2
a 2
Fg. 1 2
1.
p
f
Cor. (A) 1 2
Cl. (A)
I
Vl.
II
Vla.
Vc.
Cb.
240

244
a 2
Fl. 1 2
a 2
Fg. 1 2
a 2
Cor. (A) 1 2
Cl. (A)
tr
Vl. I
Vl. II
Vla.
Vc. Cb.
247
Solo
p

251
Fl. 1 2
Fg. 1 2
Cor. (A) 1 2
a 2
Cl. (A)
I
Vl.
II
Vla.
Vc.
Cb.
257
Fl. 1 2
Fg. 1 2
p
Cor. (A) 1 2
Cl. (A)
tr
tr
I
Vl.
tr
II
Vla.
Vc.
Cb.
p

261
Fl. 1 2
Fg. 1 2
Cor. (A) 1 2
Cl. (A)
I
Vl.
II
Vla.
Vc.
Cb.
265
Fl. 1 2
Fg. 1 2
Cor. (A) 1 2
Cl. (A)
tr
I
Vl.
II
Vla.
Vc.
Cb.

Tutti
Solo
269
Fl. 1 2
Fg. 1 2
Cor. (A) 1 2
Cl. (A)
I
Vl.
II
Vla.
Vc.
Cb.

276
Fl. 1 2
Fg. 1 2
Cor. (A) 1 2
Cl. (A)
I
Vl.
II
Vla.
Vc.
Cb.

282
Fl. 1 2
Fg. 1 2
Cor. (A) 1 2
Cl. (A)
Vl. I II
Vla.
Vc. Cb.
286
Tutti
Solo
a 2
a 2
Vc.

291
Fl. 1 2
Fg. 1 2
Cor. (A) 1 2
Cl. (A)
I
Vl.
II
Vla.
Vc.
Cb.
Tutti Bassi
p
Cb.
295
Fl. 1 2
Fg. 1 2
Cor. (A) 1 2
Cl. (A)
I
Vl.
II
Vla.
Vc.
Cb.

298
Fl. 1 2
Fg. 1 2
Cor. (A) 1 2
Cl. (A)
I
Vl.
II
Vla.
Vc.
Violoncello

302
Fl. 1 2
Fg. 1 2
Cor. (A) 1 2
Cl. (A)
I
Vl.
II
Vla.
Vc.
Vc.
Cb.
Tutti Bassi

308
Fl. 1 2
Fg. 1 2
Cor. (A) 1 2
Cl. (A)
I
Vl.
II
Vla.
Vc.
Cb.
Violoncello
Tutti Bassi

313
Fl. 1 2
Fg. 1 2
Cor. (A) 1 2
Cl. (A)
I
Vl.
II
Vla.
Vc.
Cb.

318
Fl. 1 2
Fg. 1 2
Cor. (A) 1 2
Cl. (A)
I
Vl.
II
Vla.
Vc.
Cb.
tr
p
323
Fl. 1 2
Fg. 1 2
Cor. (A) 1 2
Cl. (A)
I
Vl.
II
Vla.
Vc.
Cb.
p
p
tr

326
Fl. 1 2
Fg. 1 2
Cor. (A) 1 2
Cl. (A)
I
Vl.
II
Vla.
Vc.
Cb.

329
Fl. 1 2
Fg. 1 2
Cor. (A) 1 2
Cl. (A)
I
Vl.
II
Vla.
Vc.
Cb.
tr
tr

332
Fl. 1 2
Fg. 1 2
Cor. (A) 1 2
Cl. (A)
I
Vl.
II
Vla.
Vc.
Cb.
p
tr

335
Fl. 1 2
Fg. 1 2
Cor. (A) 1 2
Cl. (A)
I
Vl.
II
Vla.
Vc.
Cb.

338
Fl. 1 2
Fg. 1 2
Cor. (A) 1 2
Cl. (A)
I
Vl.
II
Vla.
Vc.
Cb.

341
Tutti
Fl. 1 2
Fg. 1 2
a 2
f
Cor. (A) 1 2
a 2
p
cresc.
f
Cl. (A)
tr
f
I
Vl.
II
cresc.
f
cresc.
f
Vla.
cresc.
f
Vc.
Cb.
cresc.
f

344
Fl. 1 2
f
a 2
Fg. 1 2
Cor. (A) 1 2
Cl. (A)
I
Vl.
II
Vla.
Vc.
Cb.

347
Fl. 1 2
a 2
a 2
Fg. 1 2
a 2
Cor. (A) 1 2
Cl. (A)
I
Vl.
II
Vla.
Vc.
Cb.

351
a 2
Fl. 1 2
Fg. 1 2
Cor. (A) 1 2
Cl. (A)
p
I
Vl.
II
Vla.
Vc. Cb.

356
Fl. 1 2
f
Fg. 1 2
Cor. (A) 1 2
Cl. (A)
I
Vl.
II
Vla.
Vc. Cb.

II. Adagio

Solo
Flauto 1 2
Fagotto 1 2
Corno (D) 1 2
Clarinetto principale (A)
Violino I
Violino II
Viola
Violoncello
Violoncello
Contrabbasso
p
7
Tutti
Fl. 1 2
Fg. 1 2
Cor. (D) 1 2
Cl. (A)
Vl. I
Vl. II
Vla.
Vc.
Cb.
Vc.
Tutti Bassi
f

14
Fl. 1 2
Solo
Fg. 1 2
Cor. (D) 1 2
Cl. (A)
I
Vl.
II
Vla.
Vc. Cb.
Violoncello
21
Tutti
Vc.
Tutti Bassi

28
Fl. 1 2
Solo
Fg. 1 2
a 2
Cor. (D) 1 2
Cl. (A)
I
Vl.
II
Vla.
Vc.
Cb.
p
p
p
p

35
Fl. 1 2
Fg. 1 2
Cor. (D) 1 2
Cl. (A)
I
Vl.
II
Vla.
Vc.
Cb.

40
Fl. 1 2
Fg. 1 2
Cor. (D) 1 2
p
Cl. (A)
I
Vl.
II
Vla.
Vc.
Cb.

46
Fl. 1 2
Fg. 1 2
Cor. (D) 1 2
Cl. (A)
I
Vl.
II
Vla.
Vc.
Cb.

51
Fl. 1 2
Fg. 1 2
Cor. (D) 1 2
Cl. (A)
I
Vl.
II
Vla.
Vc.
Cb.
cresc.
56
a 2
Violoncello

62
Fl. 1 2
Fg. 1 2
Cor. (D) 1 2
Cl. (A)
I
Vl.
II
Vla.
Vc.

69
Fl. 1 2
Fg. 1 2
Cor. (D) 1 2
Cl. (A)
I
Vl.
II
Vla.
Vc.
f
f

76
Tutti
Fl. 1 2
Fg. 1 2
Cor. (D) 1 2
Cl. (A)
I
Vl.
II
Vla.
Tutti Bassi
Vc.
Cb.
83
Solo
Violoncello

88
Fl. 1 2
Fg. 1 2
Cor. (D) 1 2
Cl. (A)
I
Vl.
II
Vla.
Tutti Bassi
Vc.
Cb.
p
92
Fl. 1 2
Fg. 1 2
Cor. (D) 1 2
Cl. (A)
I
Vl.
II
Vla.
Vc.
Cb.

III. Rondo

Allegro

10
Fl. 1 2
Fg. 1 2
Cor. (A) 1 2
Cl. (A)
I
Vl.
II
Vla.
Vc.
Cb.
f
p
cresc.
16
Solo

21
Fl. 1 2
Fg. 1 2
Cor. (A) 1 2
Cl. (A)
I
Vl.
II
Vla.
Violoncello
Vc.
Cb.

27
Tutti
Fl. 1 2
p
Fg. 1 2
p
Cor. (A) 1 2
Cl. (A)
I
Vl.
II
Vla.
Tutti Bassi
Vc.
Cb.
p

32
Solo
Fl. 1 2
Fg. 1 2
Cor. (A) 1 2
Cl. (A)
I
Vl.
II
Vla.
Vc. Cb.
cresc.
a 2
p cresc.
p
37
Tutti
f

42
Fl. 1 2
Solo
Fg. 1 2
a 2
Cor. (A) 1 2
a 2
Cl. (A)
Vl. I II
Vla.
Vc. Cb.
48
Tutti

54
Fl. 1 2
Solo
Fg. 1 2
a 2
Cor. (A) 1 2
Cl. (A)
I
Vl.
II
p
p
Vla.
Vc.
Cb.
61
Fl. 1 2
Fg. 1 2
Cor. (A) 1 2
Cl. (A)
I
Vl.
II
Vla.
p
Vc.
Cb.
p

67
Fl. 1 2
Fg. 1 2
Cor. (A) 1 2
Cl. (A)
I
Vl.
II
Vla.
Vc.
Cb.
73
Tutti
Solo
Fl. 1
a 2
p
Fg. 1 2
p
Cor. (A) 1 2
Cl. (A)
tr
I
Vl.
II
Vla.
Vc.
Cb.

80
Fl. 1
Fg. 1 2
Cor. (A) 1 2
Cl. (A)
I
Vl.
II
Vla.
p
Vc.
Cb.
86
Fl. 1 2
Fg. 1 2
Cor. (A) 1 2
Cl. (A)
tr
I
Vl.
II
Vla.
Vc.
Cb.

91
Fl. 1 2
Fg. 1 2
Cor. (A) 1 2
Cl. (A)
I
Vl.
II
Vla.
Vc.
Cb.
97
sfp
p

104
Fl. 1 2
Fg. 1 2
Cor. (A) 1 2
Cl. (A)
I
Vl.
II
Vla.
Vc.
Cb.
110
Fl. 1 2
Fg. 1 2
Cor. (A) 1 2
Cl. (A)
I
Vl.
II
Vla.
Vc.
Cb.

117
Fl. 1 2
Fg. 1 2
Cor. (A) 1 2
Cl. (A)
Vl. I II
Vla.
Vc. Cb.
Tutti
f
123

128
a 2
Fl. 1 2
Fg. 1 2
Cor. (A) 1 2
Cl. (A)
I
Vl.
II
Vla.
Vc.
Cb.

132
a 2
a 2
Fl. 1 2
Fg. 1 2
Cor. (A) 1 2
Cl. (A)
I
Vl.
II
Vla.
Vc.
Cb.

136
Solo
Fl. 1 2
a 2
Fg. 1 2
a 2
Cor. (A) 1 2
Cl. (A)
I
Vl.
II
Vla.
Vc.
Cb.
p
143
Fl. 1 2
Fg. 1 2
Cor. (A) 1 2
Cl. (A)
I
Vl.
II
Vla.
Vc.
Cb.

150
Fl. 1 2
Fg. 1 2
Cor. (A) 1 2
Cl. (A)
I
Vl.
II
Vla.
Vc.
Cb.
p
157
f

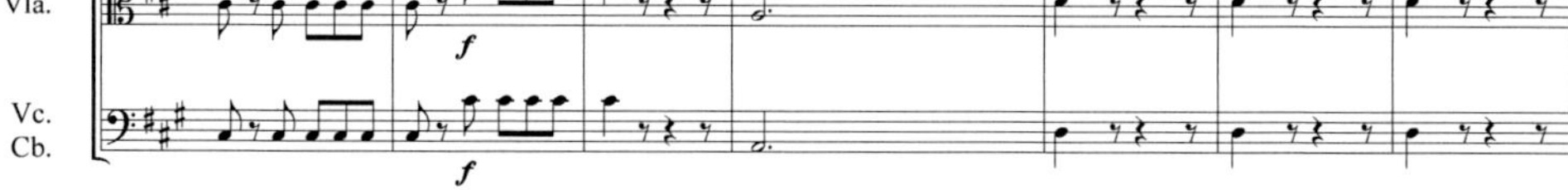
Vc.
Cb.
f

164
Fl. 1 2
p
Fg. 1 2
p
Cor. (A) 1 2
Cl. (A)
I
Vl.
II
Vla.
Vc.
Cb.
171
Fl. 1 2
Fg. 1 2
Cor. (A) 1 2
Cl. (A)
I
Vl.
II
Vla.
Vc.
Cb.

176
Fl. 1 2
Fg. 1 2
Cor. (A) 1 2
Cl. (A)
I
Vl.
II
Vla.
Vc.
Cb.
181
f

187
Fl. 1 2
Fg. 1 2
Cor. (A) 1 2
Cl. (A)
I
Vl.
II
Vla.
Vc.
Cb.
p
p
p
p
193
Fl. 1 2
Fg. 1 2
Cor. (A) 1 2
Cl. (A)
I
Vl.
II
Vla.
Vc.
Cb.

199
Fl. 1 2
Fg. 1 2
Cor. (A) 1 2
Cl. (A)
I
Vl.
II
Vla.
Violoncello
Vc.
207
Fl. 1 2
Fg. 1 2
Cor. (A) 1 2
Cl. (A)
I
Vl.
II
Vla.
Tutti Bassi
Vc.
Cb.
p

212
Fl. 1 2
Fg. 1 2
Cor. (A) 1 2
Cl. (A)
I
Vl.
II
Vla.
Violoncello
Vc.
Cb.
218
Fl. 1
Fg. 1 2
Cor. (A) 1 2
Cl. (A)
I
Vl.
II
Vla.
Vc.
Vc.
Cb.
Tutti Bassi

225
Fl. 1 2
Fg. 1 2
Cor. (A) 1 2
Cl. (A)
I
Vl.
II
Vla.
Vc.
Cb.
229
sfp
p
sfp
sfp
sfp
sfp
sfp
p

235
Fl. 1 2
sfp
Fg. 1 2
sfp
Cor. (A) 1 2
sfp
Cl. (A)
I
Vl.
II
sfp
sfp
Vla.
sfp
Vc.
Cb.
sfp
242
Fl. 1 2
Fg. 1 2
Cor. (A) 1 2
Cl. (A)
I
Vl.
II
Vla.
Vc.
Cb.

248
Fl. 1 2
Fg. 1 2
Cor. (A) 1 2
Cl. (A)
I
Vl.
II
Vla.
Vc.
Cb.
254
Tutti
p cresc.
f
cresc.
p

261
Solo
Fl. 1 2
Fg. 1 2
Cor. (A) 1 2
Cl. (A)
I
Vl.
II
Vla.
p
Vc.
Cb.
p
266
Fl. 1 2
Fg. 1 2
Cor. (A) 1 2
Cl. (A)
I
Vl.
II
Vla.
Violoncello
Vc.
Cb.

271
Fl. 1 2
Fg. 1 2
Cor. (A) 1 2
Cl. (A)
I
Vl.
II
Vla.
Vc.
Cb.
277
Tutti
p
cresc.
a 2
p cresc.
Tutti Bassi

281
Solo
Tutti
Fl. 1 2
Fg. 1 2
a 2
Cor. (A) 1 2
a 2
Cl. (A)
I
Vl.
II
Vla.
Vc.
Cb.
287
Solo
a 2
a 2

Tutti
292
Fl. 1 2
Fg. 1 2
Cor. (A) 1 2
Cl. (A)
I
Vl.
II
Vla.
Vc.
Cb.
298
Solo

303
Fl. 1 2
Fg. 1 2
Cor. (A) 1 2
Cl. (A)
I
Vl.
II
Vla.
Vc.
Cb.
308
Fl. 1 2
Fg. 1 2
Cor. (A) 1 2
Cl. (A)
I
Vl.
II
Vla.
Vc.
Cb.

312
Fl. 1 2
Fg. 1 2
Cor. (A) 1 2
Cl. (A)
tr
I
Vl.
II
Vla.
Vc.
Cb.
317
Fl. 1 2
Fg. 1 2
Cor. (A) 1 2
Cl. (A)
tr
I
Vl.
II
Vla.
Vc.
Cb.

322
Fl. 1 2
Fg. 1 2
Cor. (A) 1 2
Cl. (A)
I
Vl.
II
Vla.
Violoncello
Vc.
Cb.
327
Fl. 1 2
Fg. 1 2
Cor. (A) 1 2
Cl. (A)
I
Vl.
II
Vla.
Tutti Bassi
Vc.
Cb.

332
Fl. 1 2
Fg. 1 2
Cor. (A) 1 2
Cl. (A)
I
Vl.
II
Vla.
Vc.
Cb.
338
p
p
Violoncello
Vc.

343
Tutti
Fl. 1 2
Fg. 1 2
Cor. (A) 1 2
Cl. (A)
Vl. I II
Vla.
Vc. Cb.
cresc.
p cresc.
f
Tutti Bassi
349
a 2